QUICK GUIDE TO FANTASY SPORTS

QUICK GUIDE TO
FANTASY FOOTBALL

by Bo Mitchell

BrightPoint Press

San Diego, CA

© 2021 BrightPoint Press
an imprint of ReferencePoint Press, Inc.
Printed in the United States

For more information, contact:
BrightPoint Press
PO Box 27779
San Diego, CA 92198
www.BrightPointPress.com

ALL RIGHTS RESERVED.

No part of this work covered by the copyright hereon may be reproduced or used in any form or by any means—graphic, electronic, or mechanical, including photocopying, recording, taping, web distribution, or information storage retrieval systems—without the written permission of the publisher.

LIBRARY OF CONGRESS CATALOGING-IN-PUBLICATION DATA

Names: Mitchell, Bo, author.
Title: Quick guide to fantasy football / by Bo Mitchell.
Description: San Diego, CA : ReferencePoint Press, [2021] | Series: Quick guide to fantasy sports | Includes bibliographical references and index. | Audience: Grades 10-12
Identifiers: LCCN 2020002426 (print) | LCCN 2020002427 (eBook) | ISBN 9781678200046 (Hardcover) | ISBN 9781678200053 (eBook)
Subjects: LCSH: Fantasy football (Game)--Juvenile literature.
Classification: LCC GV1202.F34 M58 2020 (print) | LCC GV1202.F34 (eBook) | DDC 794.9/332--dc23
LC record available at https://lccn.loc.gov/2020002426
LC eBook record available at https://lccn.loc.gov/2020002427

CONTENTS

AT A GLANCE	4
INTRODUCTION	6
GETTING READY FOR FOOTBALL	
CHAPTER ONE	12
WHAT IS FANTASY FOOTBALL?	
CHAPTER TWO	24
HOW DO FANTASY FOOTBALL LEAGUES GET STARTED?	
CHAPTER THREE	42
HOW DO FANTASY FOOTBALL OWNERS PREPARE?	
CHAPTER FOUR	58
HOW DO OWNERS MANAGE A TEAM?	
Glossary	74
Source Notes	75
For Further Research	76
Index	78
Image Credits	79
About the Author	80

AT A GLANCE

- Fantasy football is a fun way for fans to enjoy the NFL and learn more about the game.

- Points are scored based on the statistics of NFL players.

- Every league has a commissioner to keep things organized.

- Leagues need to set up clear rules. Each league can customize its own.

- Many websites host fantasy football leagues.

- The fantasy football draft is the biggest day on the fantasy football calendar.

- Sources to help owners with their fantasy football teams are easy to find. They include websites, magazines, TV shows, radio shows, and podcasts.

- Participants need to set their lineups every week of the season.

- Participants can improve their teams with free agent pickups and trades.

- Staying active is vital. The game is best when all participants in a league continue to try.

INTRODUCTION

GETTING READY FOR FOOTBALL

As Landon threw the football to his buddy Evan, all he could think about was the upcoming start of the football season. "I think this is the season my Minnesota Vikings could win the Super Bowl," Landon said.

"No way!" said Evan. "The Denver Broncos are going all the way!"

Fantasy football is a great way for fans to become more involved in the sport.

As Evan fired the ball back, Landon pretended to be his favorite player, catching the pass and doing a touchdown dance.

"Adam Thielen is the best receiver in football," Landon proclaimed confidently.

"If I owned an NFL team, he would be the first player I would get."

"Over Patrick Mahomes? Or Christian McCaffrey?" asked Evan. "Nobody's better than those guys. If I owned a team, I'd make sure they were on it!"

Evan's older sister, Anna, overheard the two boys and interrupted, "Why don't you guys just join my fantasy football **league**?" she asked. "That way you can both have your very own teams and get whatever players you want. Grace said she's going to play. So are Mohammed, Sophia, Dylan,

Many people play fantasy football with their friends and family.

Austin, Olivia, and Jose. We need two more people. If you guys play, we'll have enough."

"Fantasy football… I've heard of that," said Evan. "I'll give it a try."

Fans of any NFL team can play fantasy football. They may even find new players to root for.

"Yeah, my uncle and cousin play fantasy football. They say it's a lot of fun," said Landon. "Count me in too. I'm going to make sure I get Adam Thielen!"

FANTASY FOOTBALL IS FOR ALL FANS

Fantasy football is a great hobby for fans of any age. Setting up a league is easy online. Owners can prepare using some simple strategies and tools. Once an owner has a team, the fun is just starting. Managing a team throughout the season leads to winning. Anybody can play fantasy football.

CHAPTER ONE

WHAT IS FANTASY FOOTBALL?

In fantasy football, participants earn points based on how NFL players perform. When a player gains yards or scores, his fantasy team gets points. Kickers score points too. Fantasy football isn't limited to offense. Teams have a defense. They earn points also.

The actions of NFL players on the field earn points for fantasy teams.

Every fantasy team has one game per week. They play against another team. A league with ten teams has five games every week. The team with the higher score wins. The goal is to pick the players who score a lot of points. Fantasy football is a skill game. It tests a fan's ability to predict player performance.

A GREAT WAY TO LEARN ABOUT FOOTBALL

Playing fantasy football is a great way to enjoy the sport. Fans can learn more about individual players. Many watch new teams. FantasySports.net writes, "Before starting to play fantasy football, fans usually stick to their own teams and watch only their games. They usually refrain from watching televised football matches until and unless it somehow affects their favorite team."[1]

Many people begin to follow new teams or players after joining fantasy football.

Fantasy football has made the NFL more popular. Millions of people play. Fans watch their players score points. Some watch other teams' players. That means more people are watching NFL games. Many watch several games. They look the players up online. They follow NFL news.

WHICH STATISTICS COUNT?

Fantasy football awards points for touchdowns, extra points, and field goals. Two-point conversions also earn points. Rushing yards, passing yards, and receiving yards are often counted. Sacks, interceptions, and fumble recoveries can earn points for defense. Some leagues give points based on how few points a defense allows.

ESPN.com says, "When you start pulling for your players and against the players on your opponent's team each week, you'll find a new way to enjoy watching NFL games. Suddenly, that Thursday Night Football game between two bad teams carries some meaning to you."[2]

GETTING A FANTASY FOOTBALL TEAM

A fantasy football league is a group of teams that compete against each other. Every person participating is called an "owner" or "manager." How do leagues form? It is easy to start one. Only interested people are needed. They can be friends,

Almost all leagues are online. Owners can manage their teams whenever they want.

family members, or neighbors. There are also many leagues online. Each person has a team. Owners run their teams like a real

NFL owner. They make all of the decisions. They choose players for their teams. They decide which players to use. The winning owner gets all the credit.

THE RIGHT NUMBER OF TEAMS

A league is best with ten to twelve teams. Six or eight teams may be too few. Every team will be filled with star players. Some owners find it boring. But it could be helpful for beginners. They can focus on learning the game. More than twelve teams can be too many. There might not be enough good players for everyone. This creates a bigger challenge.

Leagues need an even number of teams. Each team needs an opponent each week. The fantasy season usually lasts 13 or 14 weeks. Then each league has playoff games. Each league decides how long its season lasts.

Leagues track wins and losses. Points scored and allowed are also tracked. Points are often used as tiebreakers. This happens if teams finish with the same record. Leagues decide how teams advance to the playoffs. The playoff games determine the champion. The fantasy football playoffs take place during the final weeks of the

Fantasy teams advance to the playoffs just like real NFL teams. The final two teams compete to win the league's championship.

regular NFL season. As of 2019, the

regular NFL season has seventeen weeks.

Semifinals are held with the four best

teams. These games are usually held in Week 15. The championship is between a league's final two teams. The final game is usually played in Week 16. The winner is crowned champion.

WEEK 17

The regular NFL season lasts seventeen weeks. However, most leagues hold their championship in Week 16. There's a good reason for this. The best NFL teams often have a playoff spot clinched by Week 17. If they do, they sometimes rest their best players. That can hurt fantasy owners. Leagues find it fairer to determine the champion when all the players are still playing.

Fantasy football takes place during the regular NFL season and ends before the NFL playoffs begin.

CHAPTER TWO

HOW DO FANTASY FOOTBALL LEAGUES GET STARTED?

Setting up a league takes a few steps. First, members need to decide on the type of league. One-year leagues are the most common. They are the easiest for beginners. The league only lasts one year.

Commissioners have many jobs, including setting up the league, approving trades, and settling owner disputes.

Some fantasy football leagues last several years. These are keeper or dynasty leagues.

Someone has to be in charge of the league. That person is called a **commissioner**. The commissioner is responsible for setting up the league website. The commissioner settles disputes. Sometimes they approve trades. The commissioner also schedules the **draft**.

RUNNING A FANTASY FOOTBALL LEAGUE ONLINE

Fantasy football existed before the internet. The rules were created in 1962. The first league began in 1963. There were no websites. This made a commissioner's job much harder. They had to use a newspaper to track scores. Points were calculated by hand. It was hard work.

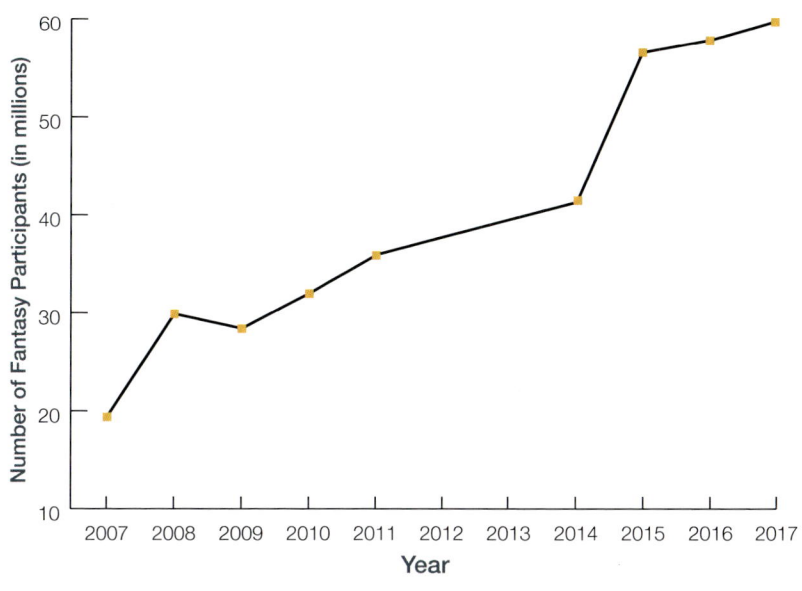

Fantasy sports have grown significantly with the rise of the internet, smartphones, and other technology. The Fantasy Sports & Gaming Association (FSGA) released a study on the number of people who play fantasy sports. According to their study, the number of fantasy players more than doubled between the years 2007 and 2017.

Fantasy football surged in popularity in the 1990s. Several websites started hosting leagues. That changed everything. Websites automatically track points. Joining a league became easier. The first league websites included Yahoo! and CBS SportsLine. Now there are many different options for leagues. ESPN.com, MyFantasyLeague.com, and NFL.com are some of the most popular sites. Leagues can use whichever they prefer. Each site has its own advantages.

    A league must agree on a website. The commissioner will add the league's rules. Most sites set a weekly schedule. Each team meets every other team at least once. A set schedule keeps the league organized. The commissioner can adjust the schedule if needed.

Different leagues have different scoring rules. Most count a touchdown run as six points. But not every league counts touchdown throws the same.

FANTASY FOOTBALL RULES

Each league sets up its own rules. There are many decisions to make. How many players does each team have? Which positions are in a starting **lineup**? Most teams have twelve to sixteen players. However, not every player's points count every week.

Teams need to have a set number of starters. The rest are kept on the bench. Only points scored by starters count. Some leagues use points scored by bench players to break ties. Owners set their starting lineups each week.

Fantasy owners want their team to score more points than their opponent's team.

In a typical league, teams have eight or nine starters. Most teams have about five bench spots. A league might require one quarterback, two running backs, two wide receivers, and one tight end. Most also require a kicker and a team defense. Many leagues include a flex position—either an extra running back or wide receiver. Some have two or more flex spots. Every league is different. Owners must agree on starting positions.

HOW TO KEEP SCORE

Early leagues used simple scoring rules. The commissioner had to do all the math. The rules could not be complicated. The basic scoring rules have stayed similar.

A touchdown run or catch is six points. This is the NFL score for a touchdown.

Some leagues score touchdown passes differently than touchdown runs or catches.

Some leagues award six points for touchdown passes. However, this gives an advantage to teams with the best quarterbacks. It makes a quarterback like Patrick Mahomes far more valuable than a running back like Ezekiel Elliott. Most leagues count a touchdown pass as three or four points. This keeps the game fair.

Kickers earn points too. Field goals usually earn three points. Some leagues award extra points for long field goals. If Greg Zuerlein boots a 55-yard field goal, that might be worth five points in some leagues. An extra point kick after a touchdown is worth one point.

As fantasy football grew, so did the number of scoring systems. Online leagues allow leagues to customize their scoring systems. Each league decides how points

AUCTIONS

An auction is another popular way to select players. It is different than having a draft. Owners nominate players for bidding. Each owner gets a set number of imaginary "dollars" to spend in a fantasy auction. Owners bid on the players. The highest bidder gets the player. Owners only have a certain amount of "money." This must be used to fill their whole team. They can use most of their budget to get stars like Michael Thomas or Lamar Jackson. If so, they won't have much money left. They will have to fill the rest of their roster with cheaper players. Once every team has enough players, the auction ends.

are earned. Some leagues prefer simple rules. Others want more complicated rules. Any point system can be used. However, owners must all agree to it. Mitchell Renz of the fantasy website Gridiron Experts says, "People want to see points; there is a satisfaction of being able to watch your team score points right in front of your eyes."[3]

Some leagues give points for receptions. These are called **point-per-reception (PPR) leagues**. "This can make a big difference in evaluating running backs, for example, because two backs who each finish with 1,500 yards from scrimmage might have different values if one catches a lot of passes and the other doesn't," wrote AJ Mass for ESPN.com.[4] Some leagues

In a PPR league, owners want running backs who catch a lot of passes.

award one point for each catch. Other leagues do half a point. Each league sets its own rules.

Consider the league's scoring system before the draft. Christian McCaffrey and

Derrick Henry are both great running backs. Both rushed for more than 1,300 yards and at least 15 touchdowns in 2019. But McCaffrey caught 116 passes. Henry caught 18. McCaffrey is far more valuable in a PPR league.

THE DRAFT

Each team needs players. Leagues need a fair way to divide players. Most hold a draft. This is done before the start of the season. A draft works similar to the NFL draft. Each team takes turns picking players.

This continues until every team has enough players. The draft order can be determined any way the league wants.

Most leagues use a snake draft order. Some leagues call it a serpentine draft. This style reverses direction after every round.

KEEPER AND DYNASTY LEAGUES

In keeper leagues, owners stay in the league several seasons. A certain number of players can be carried between seasons. A league might require fourteen players per team. Each team can keep five players from the previous year. That league only needs nine rounds in its draft. In dynasty leagues, owners can keep every player season to season.

If a league has ten teams, each round lasts ten picks. In a snake draft, the order goes from team one to team ten. In the second round, the order goes from ten to one. The third round goes one to ten again. This continues for the whole draft. It is fairer than going from one to ten every round.

The length of the draft depends on the league rules. If each team needs fourteen players, the draft last fourteen rounds. Drafts can be done online. However, it is a lot of fun to get together with other owners. This is especially true for leagues made of friends or family members. Many people

Many people consider draft day the most exciting day of fantasy football. Some leagues throw parties.

select the players in person. Draft day is

the biggest day for fantasy football. Some

leagues like to make it a party.

CHAPTER THREE

HOW DO FANTASY FOOTBALL OWNERS PREPARE?

Success in fantasy football takes a little luck. But preparation can help. Owners need to prepare for the draft. They need to know which players to pick. They also need to know when to pick them.

There are many strategies to build winning teams. Knowing which players score the most points is crucial.

LEARN ABOUT STATISTICS

Points are earned based on player performances in games. Looking at players' statistics is a good idea. Owners need to know which statistics matter.

Touchdowns and yards earn points. Owners track who scored touchdowns. They learn who had the most yards. Leagues use different stats. It is important to know which ones affect your league. For example, owners in a PPR league need to know who caught the most passes.

Players' stats change between seasons. Aaron Jones scored 16 touchdowns in 2019. But that doesn't mean he will do the same in 2020. Owners predict who will have the best statistics. Players with consistently good statistics are valuable. How do owners predict stats?

Owners follow NFL and fantasy news and track player statistics to see who would be a good fit for their teams.

FOLLOW THE NEWS

It is important to understand why players perform well or poorly. Were they injured? Did they miss games? Were they on a good team or a bad team? Did a quarterback have good stats because he had good receivers? Have any of those factors changed? The NFL changes between seasons. Players change teams. New players enter through the NFL Draft each spring. It is important to follow football news. Owners should follow potential players. Fantasy football isn't just for fans who know a lot about the NFL. It's also

AVERAGE DRAFT POSITION

When preparing for a draft, it's good to know when players are usually selected. The Average Draft Position (ADP) of players uses data from actual drafts. The ADP data tracks when players are drafted. It's an accurate way to gauge the value of players. This information helps owners time their draft picks. They can avoid taking players too soon or late. Owners can find up-to-date ADP data on many websites.

for those who want to learn. Owners want as much information as possible. It makes predicting player statistics easier.

The sources for news and analysis are endless. Many websites are dedicated to fantasy football. Social media can be

Some players are more valuable than others. Cheat sheets help owners determine who is most likely to be a strong player.

a good resource. Many owners follow NFL reporters or analysts online. Fantasy football radio shows, television shows, and podcasts have become quite popular. Some experts recommend fantasy football magazines. Many resources come out before the season begins.

CHOOSING THE RIGHT PLAYERS

Fantasy football media is full of useful information. These sources also help owners learn the best ways to play. Many offer tools to make drafting a team easier. The most important tool for any draft is a **cheat sheet**.

A cheat sheet ranks each player. Cheat sheets sort players by position. The most valuable players are listed at the top. The value of players can vary. Each sheet is based on the opinions of whoever published it. No two cheat sheets will look exactly alike. But owners will see similarities between cheat sheets. The same names will tend to be toward the top.

A cheat sheet is helpful during a draft. As the players get selected, owners mark them off. This tells them which players have been taken. It makes it easier to see who is still available. Cheat sheets are not just

Using tools such as cheat sheets to keep track of already selected players helps a draft go smoothly.

for beginners. Even owners who have been playing for twenty years use cheat sheets. Fantasy football websites and magazines have cheat sheets available. Experts create cheat sheets for different scoring systems. Players can find one for their league's rules. For example, there are cheat sheets designed specifically for PPR leagues.

Cheat sheets aren't the only resource. Many sources publish **mock drafts**.

MOCK DRAFTS

Owners can do more than look at expert mock drafts. Many owners take part in mock drafts. It's another good way to get ready for a real draft. The purpose is to get a good idea of where players are being selected. Picking from different spots in the draft order can be very helpful. Owners can practice against other owners from all over the world. Many websites run free mock drafts.

Mock drafts are pretend drafts. These are done by experts. They suggest when to select players. Rankings can be confusing. Mock drafts show what they mean. Owners can see rankings applied to a draft. Mock drafts show where positions are often filled. Owners can use them to make a plan.

People use different strategies. However, experts often follow patterns. Most draft running backs and receivers early. They leave kickers and defensive teams for later. There are few elite running backs and receivers. The difference between their statistics and those of other running backs

An owner who is prepared is more likely to have a successful draft.

and receivers is huge. Kickers and defenses can be high scoring too. But the difference between an elite kicker and a so-so kicker is small. It may only be a point or two per game. The same is true for defenses.

So the best owners use their early picks on running backs and receivers. These players have more of an impact. Then they fill other positions. Experts find these strategies successful. It is a good plan for beginners.

HAVING A SUCCESSFUL DRAFT

After choosing a cheat sheet, an owner is ready to draft their team. Good owners pay attention. It is important to track which players were selected. They also watch other teams. This includes the positions of players chosen and which positions opponents still need. If drafting online, the website will track this information.

Fantasy owners should be proud of their teams. They spend a whole season managing it. They should like their choices. "Every pick should be your own," says Vinnie Iyer of Sporting News. "Don't base it on what everyone is doing because you think that's what you should be doing."[5] Even if an expert suggests drafting a player in the tenth round, owners aren't required to follow that advice. The experts are there to help owners be successful. But owners should not be afraid to trust their instincts.

Fantasy football is more fun with a few favorite players on the team. "Listen to all

Most fantasy owners try to draft some of their favorite NFL players.

you respect, but make your own decisions," says Scott Pianowski of Yahoo! Sports. "It's YOUR team. You're the guy or girl who has to like it."[6] Drafting a good team is just the start of the work for owners though. Decisions need to be made throughout the season.

CHAPTER FOUR

HOW DO OWNERS MANAGE A TEAM?

The teams have been drafted. Now what? Having a successful draft is important. However, owners still have work to do. Only some players start. The biggest job owners have each week is setting their starting lineups.

Owners must set their starting lineups every week before games begin.

SETTING A FANTASY FOOTBALL LINEUP

Sometimes it's easy to decide which players to start and which to bench. The best players should start almost every week.

This is unless they are injured or if their team has a bye week. However, not all players are automatic starters. Picking between two players can be difficult. Owners should look at the defenses the players will be facing. For example, an owner choosing a running back should look at how well the opposing defenses stop the run.

These statistics can be easily found online. One source is the FFToday website. The player facing the tougher defense should be on the bench. However, not all decisions work out. Even great players have bad games. Owners who make

Real NFL teams have backup players in case of poor performance or injuries. Fantasy owners can add and drop players.

well-informed lineup decisions have the most success.

FREE AGENTS

Fantasy football owners don't need to keep players all season. Players get hurt. Sometimes they don't play well. Owners can change their teams. Players who didn't get drafted are available to replace players. Available players are called **free agents**. Every league has rules about adding free agents.

Owners cannot just keep adding players. For each player added, one needs to be dropped. Some leagues allow teams with

An owner's roster can only have a certain number of players. Owners must select a player to drop if they want to add a new one.

the worst records to add players first. Those with the best records are last in line. This is how early fantasy football leagues used to work. Some still do because it's simple.

Owners follow their players' performances to see if they are doing well or need to be cut.

A more popular way to add players is an auction. This method is made easier by the internet. Each team has a free agent acquisition budget (FAAB). FAAB is fake money that owners can spend on free agents. Throughout the season, owners submit bids. Bids are usually submitted on the league website on Tuesdays. The auction is typically blind. This means nobody knows what other owners bid. On Wednesday, the winning bids are revealed.

If an owner didn't win, they can still add players. Leagues usually allow additional players to be added for free

Owners use trades to acquire strong players who have already been drafted by another team.

after the auction. This is usually done on a first-come, first-served basis. The first owner to pick a player gets that player. Commissioners can set up the league rules on the website.

FREE AGENCY DECISIONS

Adding and dropping players is vital to success. Owners pay attention through the season. Understanding which players to replace is important. So is knowing when to replace someone. Poor performance and injuries are the main reason owners replace players. They also need to know which free agents are playing well. Knowing who to pick up is part of the puzzle. Players who perform well in several games are valuable. "Beware of one-week wonders," warns Martin Signore in his book, *Fantasy Football for Dummies*. "Each week, many lesser-known players have big games,

> **BYE WEEKS**
>
> Owners need to watch out for bye weeks in the NFL schedule. NFL teams do not play during a bye. They have a week off to rest. Byes can make it difficult to set a lineup. Looking ahead at the NFL schedule is important. Owners must avoid having too many players on bye weeks at the same time.

but you must decide the odds of those performances happening again."[7] Sammy Watkins scored three touchdowns in the Chiefs' first game of the 2019 season. Many fantasy owners rushed to add him. But Watkins did not score another touchdown the rest of the season. Adding a free agent doesn't have to be a permanent decision. Sometimes one doesn't work out. An owner can find someone new the next week.

MAKING FANTASY FOOTBALL TRADES

Owners can add players through trades. This is a process where teams exchange players. Trades are less common than adding free agents. They have benefits over free agents. Owners can usually get a better player through a trade. But trades have their drawbacks. Most owners have to trade a good player to get one in return. Trades aren't always one-for-one exchanges. Some trades involve two or three players exchanged for one. Some trades have several players going both ways. In keeper and dynasty leagues, owners can include future draft picks, just like real NFL teams. Exploring different kinds of trades is part of the fun.

TRADING STRATEGIES

There's an old saying that goes, "Buy low, sell high." It is usually used in business. However, it's a good strategy for trading. When a player has some poor games, his value is low. An owner might be more likely to trade him. When a player has good stats, his value is high. An owner can get more by trading him.

STAYING ACTIVE

Fantasy football owners need to keep trying. It doesn't matter how their team is doing. All teams have bad weeks. Setting weekly lineups is necessary. This is especially important close to the playoffs. As an article

Fantasy football is about having fun and finding new ways to enjoy the NFL.

on ESPN.com points out, "Put yourself in the shoes of a manager who is competing for the final playoff spot with the team facing someone who has thrown in the towel already. If he/she tanks the game by not doing his/her part, it could affect the outcome of the entire season."[8] Fantasy football should be fun. It's more fun when everyone tries their best.

GLOSSARY

cheat sheet

A ranking of players, sorted by position, to help owners in fantasy football drafts.

commissioner

The person in charge of organizing a fantasy football league.

draft

The most popular way for owners to select players for their fantasy football teams.

free agent

NFL players who aren't on a league's fantasy football team.

league

A group of fantasy football teams that play against each other.

lineup

The players on a fantasy football team that start in a given week of the season.

mock draft

Practice drafts used as a tool to help owners prepare for their real draft.

SOURCE NOTES

CHAPTER ONE: WHAT IS FANTASY FOOTBALL?

1. "Fantasy Football – Everything Beginners Need to Know," *Fantasy Sports,* n.d. www.fantasysports.net.

2. "ESPN Fantasy Football 101: How to Play," *ESPN.com,* August 5, 2017. www.espn.com.

CHAPTER TWO: HOW DO FANTASY FOOTBALL LEAGUES GET STARTED?

3. Mitchell Renz. "Fantasy Football Commissioner Tips: How to Run a Great League," *Gridiron Experts, July 12, 2017.* gridironexperts.com.

4. AJ Mass, "How to Play Fantasy Football," *ESPN.com*, June 24, 2014. http://www.espn.com/.

CHAPTER THREE: HOW DO FANTASY FOOTBALL OWNERS PREPARE?

5. Scott Pianowski, "Your 2019 Fantasy Football Cliff Notes: Last-Minute Draft Tips," *Yahoo! Sports*, August 30, 2019. sports.yahoo.com.

6. Vinnie Iyer, "Fantasy Football Draft Strategy: Tips, Advice for Dominating Your 2019 Snake Draft," *Sporting News,* September 3, 2019. www.sportingnews.com.

CHAPTER FOUR: HOW DO OWNERS MANAGE A TEAM?

7. Martin Signore. "Fantasy Football for Dummies Cheat Sheet," *Dummies,* n.d. www.dummies.com.

8. "Fantasy Football 101: Fantasy Football Etiquette," *ESPN.com,* June 8, 2017. www.espn.com.

FOR FURTHER RESEARCH

BOOKS

James Buckley Jr., *Fantasy Football.* Broomall, PA: Mason Crest, 2017.

Matt Doeden, *Fantasy Football Math: Using Stats to Score Big in Your League.* Mankato, MN: Capstone Press, 2017.

Barry Wilner, *Great Football Debates.* Minneapolis, MN: Abdo Publishing, 2019.

INTERNET SOURCES

Alex Gelhar, "How to Play Fantasy Football: A Beginner's Guide," *NFL*, August 8, 2017. www.nfl.com.

"Fantasy Football Cheat Sheet Central," *ESPN.com*, September 5, 2019. www.espn.com.

"Fantasy Football Draft Simulator," *Fantasy Pros*, n.d. www.draftwizard.fantasypros.com.

WEBSITES

ESPN.com
www.espn.com

ESPN.com features fantasy sports information, articles by experts, cheat sheets, mock drafts, and a league hosting service.

NFL.com
www.nfl.com

NFL.com is the National Football League's official website and includes football news and player statistics.

Yahoo! Fantasy
football.fantasysports.yahoo.com

Yahoo! has a popular fantasy football league hosting service as well as breaking news and analysis from around the NFL.

INDEX

auction, 35, 65–67
Average Draft Position (ADP), 47

bench, 30–31, 59–60

cheat sheet, 49–52, 55
commissioner, 4, 26, 28, 32, 67

draft, 4, 26, 35, 37–41, 42, 47, 49–53, 55–57, 58, 62, 70
dynasty league, 25, 39, 70

Elliott, Ezekiel, 34

free agent, 5, 62–65, 67–70
free agent acquisition budget (FAAB), 65

Henry, Derrick, 38

Iyer, Vinnie, 56

Jackson, Lamar, 35
Jones, Aaron, 44

keeper league, 25, 39, 70

Mahomes, Patrick, 8, 33
Mass, AJ, 36
McCaffrey, Christian, 8, 37–38
mock draft, 52–53

Pianowski, Scott, 57
playoffs, 20, 22, 71–73
Point-Per-Reception (PPR) league, 36–38, 44, 52

Renz, Mitchell, 35–36

Signore, Martin, 68

Thielen, Adam, 7, 11
Thomas, Michael, 35
trades, 5, 26, 69–70, 71

Watkins, Sammy, 69

Zuerlein, Greg, 34

IMAGE CREDITS

Cover: © Mitch Gunn/
Shutterstock Images
5: © ESB Professional/
Shutterstock Images
7: © Arena Creative/
Shutterstock Images
9: © Monkey Business Images/
Shutterstock Images
10: © Joseph Sohm/
Shutterstock Images
13: © Mitch Gunn/Shutterstock Images
15: © Prostock-Studio/iStockphoto
18: © tsyhun/Shutterstock Images
21: © undefined undefined/
iStockphoto
23: © Alexey Stiop/
Shutterstock Images
25: © Monkey Business Images/
Shutterstock Images
27: © Red Line Editorial
29: © Jamie Lamor Thompson/
Shutterstock Images
31: © David Lee/Shutterstock Images
33: © Jamie Lamor Thompson/
Shutterstock Images
37: © Steve Jacobson/
Shutterstock Images
41: © Gorodenkoff/
Shutterstock Images
43: © Action Sports Photography/
Shutterstock Images
45: © Jacob Lund/
Shutterstock Images
48: © G. Newman Lowrance/
AP Images
51: © Al Behrman/AP Images
54: © fizkes/Shutterstock Images
57: © Mitch Gunn/Shutterstock Images
59: © Monkey Business Images/
Shutterstock Images
61: © Mitch Gunn/Shutterstock Images
63: © SDI Productions/iStockphoto
64: © Ken Durden/
Shutterstock Images
66: © Mike Roemer/AP Images
72: © Wpadington/
Shutterstock Images

ABOUT THE AUTHOR

Bo Mitchell has lived in Minnesota his entire life and graduated from the University of Minnesota in Minneapolis. He started playing fantasy football in 1988 and then started writing about sports professionally in 1993. Bo has cohosted fantasy football radio shows and podcasts. He has also authored several educational books about sports and written about sports for magazines and many websites.